The FIRST BOOK of
BRAZIL

The church of San Francisco Convent, Salvador

The FIRST BOOK of

BRAZIL

by Sally Sheppard

ILLUSTRATED WITH PHOTOGRAPHS

FRANKLIN WATTS, INC.

575 Lexington Avenue • New York 22

Library of Congress Catalog Card Number: 61-9739
© Copyright 1962 by Franklin Watts, Inc.
Printed in the United States of America
by Polygraphic Company of America, Inc.

5 6

Contents

Brazil, a Pioneer Nation   1

The Land   3

Brazil's History   6

The People   15

Brazil's Music and Art   27

Coffee Galore   31

A Variety of Products   36

The Rubber Boom — and Its End   41

Some Cities of Brazil   42

Brazil Moves West   61

Carnival   67

Religious and National Holidays   70

A Glimpse into a Wilderness   74

Index   81

HESS — CUSHING

View of Sugar Loaf, Rio de Janeiro

Brazil, a Pioneer Nation

THERE ARE probably few modern nations in the world today where the pioneer spirit is more alive than in Brazil. Although the country was discovered by the Portuguese more than four hundred years ago, until recent times the opening up of much of its inland territory was difficult and often impossible, even for the hardiest pioneers.

There are many reasons for this. Along more than half the seacoast are mountains, themselves a barrier. They cause most of Brazil's many rivers to drop toward the sea in swift rapids and falls. In the past, carrying canoes and supplies around these unnavigable places was impractical because of the dense jungles and swamplands.

Before the days of modern road-building machinery, roads had to be hacked through the forests by hand. This primitive method took hundreds of men, who had to be fed and cared for while the work went on. If settlements were to be made, moreover, the settlers had to plan on carrying enough supplies to last until land could be cleared and crops planted and harvested.

In addition, the pioneers had to face the dangers of wild animals and poisonous snakes and insects. Yellow fever, malaria, and other tropical diseases took the lives of many explorers and discouraged other would-be pioneers from leaving the safety and comforts of the coastal cities.

Because of all these drawbacks the vast interior of Brazil had been little developed until the twentieth century. Today, however, there are airplanes and radios and heavy machinery — bulldozers, cranes, and tractors. With them, the wilderness is easier to conquer. Young men and women can begin an exciting new existence

1

Jungle road building in modern Brazil

in the interior of Brazil, knowing that only a day or two of travel by jeep will bring them to a settlement where a grassy airstrip has been cleared. If a sick child should need to be taken to a hospital, a message by short-wave radio will bring an airplane to fetch the patient. Medical supplies, mail, newspapers, food, and clothing can all be delivered by air to twentieth-century Brazilian pioneers. They need no longer be cut off from the rest of the world.

But even though nowadays thousands of Brazilians are moving westward, it will still be many years before the country's interior is fully developed. Settling new territory is still hard work and

2

the rewards of pioneering come slowly. The vast Amazon Basin and the Mato Grosso region present problems that even modern engineering finds difficult to solve completely. But everyone is working hard to fulfill former President Juscelino Kubitschek's motto: "Fifty years of progress in five."

The Land

BRAZIL, or more properly, the United States of Brazil, is the largest of the South American republics. It has 21 states, a federal district, and five territories. The country stretches about 4,889 miles along the Atlantic Ocean from north of the equator to the tiny republic of Uruguay, which is south of the equator. Brazil is the fifth largest country in the world. Only Russia, China, Canada, and the United States of America are larger. Brazil's western and northern boundaries touch all the other South American countries except Chile and Ecuador.

Brazil is shaped roughly like a triangle, as wide as it is long. Almost all of the country lies in the Tropical Zone, but it is by no means one huge jungle. The climate and landscape vary greatly throughout Brazil.

About one half the country contains the tropical rain forest of the Amazon River Basin. This lowland area is humid and hot, with dense forests, parts of which are still unexplored by white men.

The eastern section of Brazil is an enormous highland plateau with a narrow strip of coastal plain running along the Atlantic Ocean. Beginning at the northeastern port city of Salvador, the coastline rises sharply to form the beginning of the Great Escarpment, a natural mountain barrier separating the coastal settlements from the interior.

3

Iguassu Falls, at the borders of Brazil, Paraguay, and Argentina

5

Inland from the tropical seacoast, the hilly highlands stretch west into rolling prairies of fertile grassland dotted here and there with small pine forests. These grasslands are called *campos*, and it is here that the Brazilian cowboys, or *gauchos*, raise their herds of beef cattle.

There are many thousands of miles of rivers, lakes, and streams in Brazil. Some of the world's largest and most beautiful waterfalls are found in the rivers. The roar of Iguassu Falls is deafening as the water rushes over a cascade of rock more than two hundred feet high and nine hundred feet wide. These falls are surrounded by tropical forests full of orchids and are located at the point where the boundaries of Brazil, Argentina, and Paraguay meet.

A few hours by boat from the São Francisco River town of Penedo are the Falls of Paulo Afonso. They tumble almost three hundred feet into a deep gorge, densely forested. One hundred and ninety-five miles from the sea, they are the site of a large power station which supplies electricity to the cities of Salvador to the south and Recife to the north.

Brazil is rich in natural resources, but much of this wealth has yet to be made use of. Until recently, roads and railroads were few and far between. Today, however, road building, railroad construction, and the building of airports are progressing rapidly. Soon the natural materials of the interior can be transported in large amounts to the factories of the coastal region for manufacturing into products of various kinds.

Brazil's History

On April 22, 1500, just eight years after Christopher Columbus set sail from Spain and found the New World, a Portuguese explorer,

Pedro Alvares Cabral, discovered and claimed for his country the land which today is the United States of Brazil.

When Cabral set out from Portugal with thirteen ships and fifteen hundred men he was headed for the rich spice lands of India, which he meant to conquer for his king and country. Eager to make the trip around the tip of Africa to India in the shortest possible time, Cabral sailed his ships far west of the African coast in order to pick up stronger breezes. Shifting off course to the west, the Portuguese sailors soon noticed signs of land. Small tree trunks and scraps of vegetation floated on the water, while birds swooped over the waves in the distance.

Cabral, like most explorers, was a curious man. In order to see what this nearby land was like, he gave orders to sail due west. The next day, Easter Sunday, a small island was sighted in a bay near what is today the port of Salvador, the capital of the state of Bahia.

For several days small groups of sailors explored the new land, which Cabral christened Terra da Vera Cruz (Land of the True Cross). They found the mainland inhabited by Indians with dark, reddish-brown skin and shiny, smooth black hair. The Indians were short but well proportioned, and wore little except a few feathers around their heads and waists. Their bodies were colorfully decorated with vegetable dye paint. The Portuguese sailors found the Indians friendly and curious to observe the white man's ways.

Nine days after the discovery, Cabral left to complete his voyage to India. Two men were left behind in the new land, and one ship hurried back to Portugal to report the discovery to the King of Portugal. This ship took back a few Indian utensils, plants, some brilliantly colored parrots, and some logs of a highly prized wood known in Portugal as *pau-brasil*. Brazil got its name from this

7

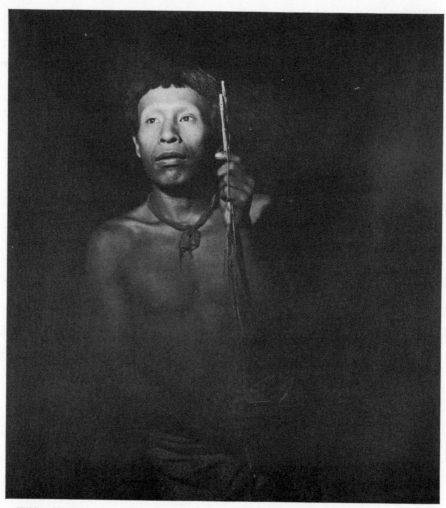

A Bororo Indian, Mato Grosso

wood, from which a red dye was extracted. In the early days of the country, brazilwood was an important item of trade with Europe.

The King of Portugal was disappointed because the explorers had heard nothing from the natives of riches such as gold or precious gems. For the next thirty years, except for infrequent trips to collect brazilwood, the Portuguese paid little attention to the land Cabral had claimed.

Since the Portuguese king seemed to care so little for his new possession, expeditions from other European countries began exploring the land and trading with the Indians. Finally the Portuguese king realized that he was in danger of losing his lands across the sea and he decided to set up a colony in Brazil.

In 1530 the Portuguese nobleman Martim Affonso de Sousa landed in Brazil with a group of soldiers and settlers. He founded the first colony on the southern coast. Today it is known as Santos, the greatest coffee port in the world.

When the King of Portugal died in 1580, neighboring Spain seized the throne. For eighty years Philip II of Spain ruled Portugal and its colonies, including Brazil. By the time Portugal had won back her throne from the Spaniards, the armies of Napoleon were racing across Europe. In 1807, when it became certain that the French armies would invade Portugal, King John VI and his court decided to flee to Brazil.

After a short stay in Bahia, where he founded Brazil's first school of medicine, the king and his family and court moved to Rio de Janeiro. One of the king's first acts was to declare the ports of Brazil open for trade to ships of all nations. A period of prosperity followed, but when the British succeeded in defeating Napoleon, King John VI was forced to return to Portugal. He left his son Pedro in charge of the Brazilian colony, warning him that Brazil

HESS — CUSHING

A vaqueiro of Marajo Island, in his poncho

10

might soon seek independence from the mother country. The wise king said to his son, "If this happens, place the crown on your head, before some adventurer gets his hands on it."

Pedro I was a popular monarch and when the government of Portugal ordered him to return there, the people of Brazil begged him to remain as their ruler. Pedro decided to stay in Brazil and named a famous scientist, José Bonifácio de Andrada e Silva, as his prime minister.

The young prince's decision made the Portuguese very angry. The *cortes*, or parliament, in Portugal demanded that Pedro fire his ministers and accept ministers from Portugal. In 1822, Pedro answered by declaring Brazil's independence from the mother country. The Brazilian people thronged the streets of Rio de Janeiro and proclaimed Pedro I their emperor.

Unfortunately the reign of Pedro I was beset by wars with the neighboring Spanish colonies. Equally unsettling to the emperor was the news from Portugal that his brother, Dom Miguel, was about to seize the throne from Maria II. Maria was Pedro's daughter and the rightful queen of Portugal. Finally Pedro I abdicated his throne to his son, Pedro II, a little boy of five years. José Bonifácio was chosen as guardian and tutor for the young prince.

As Pedro II grew up, he so impressed the ministers of state with his intelligence and good character that they decided to proclaim him emperor when he was only fifteen years old.

For fifty years Pedro II ruled Brazil, abolishing slavery and encouraging immigration from Germany and Italy. He was well liked and his reign was beneficial to the people, but the popularity of kings was declining throughout the world. France had become a republic through revolution and the United States of America was progressing by leaps and bounds under a democratic, constitu-

11

A woman of the interior, selling produce at market

12

tional government. In addition, most of Brazil's South American neighbors had declared independence from Spain and had set up republics.

Although most republican-minded Brazilians had no desire to overthrow Pedro II, some disgruntled high-ranking army officers managed his overthrow in 1889. Pedro II was exiled to Portugal with all his family, and he died in Paris a few years later.

Brazil was declared a republic by General Deodoro da Fonseca, who became provisional head of the government until free elections were held two years later. From 1891 until 1930 presidents were elected every four years.

In 1930, dissatisfaction grew among the people because of the rising cost of living, and hardships caused by the fall in price of Brazil's most important export, coffee. A revolution took place. Senhor Getulio Vargas, leader of the revolution, became president and eventually dictator of Brazil. The Vargas dictatorship lasted, with one brief interruption, until 1954, when the Brazilians again began to voice disapproval of their government. On August 24, 1954, Vargas finally shot himself.

After a hotly contested election, Juscelino Kubitschek, grandson of a Czech immigrant, and a doctor of medicine, was elected President of the United States of Brazil. Juscelino, as everyone called him, promised the people "fifty years of progress in five," with his main goal the opening of the western frontier and the building of the new capital, Brasilia. Much was accomplished under his administration: the capital came into being; thousands of miles of roads and railroads were built; airports, houses, schools, and hospitals sprang up rapidly all over the country. Government spending made prices rise, however, and today life in Brazil is very expensive, especially in the cities.

13

In October, 1960, Senhor Janio Quadros of the state of São Paulo was elected President of Brazil. Quadros was once the governor of São Paulo and was considered responsible for much of the progress and industrialization in that area. He promised the people of Brazil that he would carry on in the new Brazilian spirit of "westward ho!"

But after seven months, President Quadros resigned and left his country for England. He gave as his reason for resigning that there was too little cooperation from government officials, and claimed that certain groups within his country were interfering with his plans to put Brazil on a sound financial basis.

A clearing in the Amazon River jungle

Quadros's resignation created a political crisis in Brazil because the Vice President, João Goulart, was opposed by many conservative people. Goulart was permitted to become President, however, but was not given the power that Quadros had enjoyed. The constitution was changed so that a Premier was elected by the Congress, and the Presidency became a much less powerful office. But in 1963 the constitution was again changed, and Brazil has returned to its former presidential form of government.

The People

THE PEOPLE of Brazil are of many different races and religious beliefs, but everyone is treated alike, regardless of his religion or the color of his skin. The Brazilians are proud of their democratic behavior, and it is difficult for them to understand why in some other countries men are separated from their countrymen because of race or creed.

The original inhabitants of Brazil were the Tupi-Guarani Indians. For the most part they were peaceful people whose men fished, and hunted with bow and arrow. The women of the tribe did the farming and took care of the children.

Because few women came from Portugal with the early settlers, many of the Portuguese men married Indian women. Today there are few pure-bred Indians left in Brazil except in the most remote areas.

The Indians were friendly to the first colonists, but when the Portuguese tried to make slaves of them, trouble came. The Indians fought the white men.

When the colonists could no longer depend on Indian help for the sugar plantations and other large farms, they began to send to Africa for slaves. Most of the Negro slaves who came from Africa to the northern state of Bahia were Sudanese — tall, handsome, in-

A Marajo Islander, harpooning fish

16

HESS — CUSHING

A Japanese temple in the interior

telligent people, many of whom could read and write. Most of the other Africans taken to Brazil were from Nigeria in West Africa. As the African slaves became free, they began to mix with their white neighbors, and many of them intermarried. Today most of the Brazilian people are of mixed blood. People of mixed Indian and white blood are called *caboclos*, and most of them are very proud of their Indian ancestry.

Although most Brazilians belong to the Roman Catholic Church, there are Protestant churches and Jewish synagogues in Brazil. The country's constitution, patterned after that of the United States, insists that Church and State be separate.

Brazil is the only Latin-American country where Portuguese is the national language. Most educated people of Brazil speak Spanish as well, and many of them also speak French and English. German and Italian can be heard, too, particularly in the South where many of the immigrants have come from Germany and Italy. More than 200,000 Japanese farmers settled in Brazil during the 1930's, and they have done much to improve the land. Most of them have kept to themselves, and have not intermarried with Brazilians.

There are many different ways of life in Brazil. People of the Amazon, for instance, live quite differently from the *gauchos*, or cowboys, of the south and central plains. The Amazon people rarely stay long in one place. They like to wander, one year gathering rubber, another year building a small house in a river jungle community and fishing, hunting, and raising food for their families — or perhaps helping to harvest the year's crop of Brazil nuts.

Many of the Brazilians who live along the seacoast are fishermen. Their boats are really rafts of logs lashed together, called *jangadas*. When the fishing fleets put out to sea, their large, triangular, cotton sails billow out in the wind as the *jangadas* ride the

18

Children of a Japanese farmer, shelling beans

HESS — CUSHING

Jangadas, leaving for the fishing grounds

waves. Usually several men sail together and stay at sea for three or four days at a time. The fish are caught in large nets and put into huge wicker baskets. For anchors, the fishermen use large, heavy stones tied with seaweed. Since there are no sides to the rafts, the sailors must be sure-footed and must handle their rafts with great skill in order to keep from being swept into the sea by the rough waves.

Throughout the Brazilian countryside there are houses made of "wattle-and-daub" — that is, of sticks and twigs woven together, with the holes filled up with mud. The roofs of these houses are thatched with straw, and the floors are usually the bare ground. Many of the houses have no windows and have only one or two rooms.

Close-up of a jangada's equipment: large basket for fish, barrel for drinking water

HESS — CUSHING

A buyer examines a sleeping hammock

22

As elsewhere in the world, however, a man's house often reflects his wealth and position. Those rural people who have the materials and the necessary skills make their houses of brick or masonry. If they live in lowlands, near rivers that are likely to overflow, they protect their homes by building them on stilts. Sometimes roofs are tiled. The more prosperous farmers may have large comfortable houses with running water, electricity, and a telephone.

The furniture of the country people is simple: a few crude chairs and tables, and a floor matting of sugar-cane leaves. The usual kind of bed in the interior of Brazil is a woven cotton hammock, which is hung between two walls or posts. If a person does not sleep stretched slightly crosswise on it, he is likely to find himself suddenly spilled to the floor.

Although life in the remote interior of Brazil is fairly primitive, the cities are completely modern, with comfortable and sometimes luxurious hotels, skyscraper office buildings, and beautiful houses and apartment buildings.

In the south and southwest cattle country the cowboys, or *gauchos*, spend their days in the saddle. When they are off their horses they rarely sit down, but seem to prefer to squat as though still on horseback. The *gauchos'* children learn to ride almost before they can walk.

The grassland ranges of Brazil often become very cold at night, and a chilly wind is likely to whistle across the prairie. To keep warm on the range, the *gaucho* wears heavy leather chaps, baggy trousers which he calls *bombachas*, and a poncho, which is a heavy wool blanket with a hole in the middle through which he puts his head.

Although Brazil grows more coffee than any other country in the world, the *gaucho* prefers to drink a native tea called *herva maté*.

23

Gauchos breaking a horse, southern Brazil

(In Spanish it is spelled *yerba maté*, and many people call it Paraguay tea.) Wherever he travels, the *gaucho* carries with him a pouch of maté tea, a small gourd, and a silver tube — a kind of sipping straw. The silver tube is fashioned with a ladle at the bottom which has tiny holes so that the tea may be sucked up while the leaves are strained out. The *gaucho* brews his tea with boiling water in the gourd and drinks it through his silver straw. He is not alone in his fondness for maté tea. Brazilians in all walks of life drink it regularly.

Three foods are eaten in all parts of Brazil: rice, black beans, and manioc, a tropical root which is poison if eaten raw, but edible after it has been dried out by baking. The Brazilians make flour, bread, and a mush from manioc. They raise corn, or maize, but they prefer rice, which they also grow. Large quantities of wheat are also raised in Brazil.

Chicken, meat, and fish are eaten throughout the country, but many of the people in the pioneer land of the West eat only the wild meat and fish which they can hunt. Many little half-wild pigs with short, pointed snouts and long, bristly coats are kept by people in the interior. These pigs are usually saved for special occasions and are often barbecued over open fires.

Brazilians are fond of hot, spicy food. They have inherited this taste from their Portuguese ancestors, who brought exotic spices from India and the Far East. In the coastal towns, fish dishes are popular and the meat of the sea turtle is considered a great treat. On the cattle ranches the *gauchos* celebrate special occasions by barbecuing the meat of calves or lambs over live coals. In the state of Minas Gerais the main dish is a combination of boiled black beans, sausage, lard, bacon, ham, and orange slices all cooked together with plenty of hot pepper.

HESS — CUSHING

Dwelling house on a cattle ranch

26

Families are large in Brazil, and it is not unusual for a man and his wife to have as many as a dozen children. The children are polite and well-mannered, for while their parents give them a great deal of affection they are also very strict.

In Brazil the father is the head of the household. He makes all important decisions and handles the money. A married woman may have an outside job, but her first and most important one is to take care of her husband, her children, and her house. Girls marry when they are very young, and in some of the rural areas marriages are still arranged by the parents of the young people.

Brazil's Music and Art

BRAZILIANS are gay and friendly people, and all of them love melody and rhythm. Dancing is a favorite pastime of young and old. Their music is a blending of the native Indian, the African, and the European — like the people themselves. In it one hears the click of the castanets and the swing of the rhythms of old Spain and Portugal, together with the beat of the drums of Africa and the Brazilian jungle.

Not only has Brazil contributed its lively folk music and popular music to other countries, but two modern Brazilian composers, Heitor Villa-Lobos and Carmargo Guarnieri, have had their compositions played by most of the major symphony orchestras and soloists of the world.

The most famous modern Brazilian painter is Candido Portinari, whose murals of Latin America are in the Library of Congress in Washington, D.C., as well as in public buildings in his own country. But in Brazil perhaps the most famous of all Brazilian artists is Aleijadinho, the "Little Cripple," whose given name was Antonio Francisco Lisboa.

Detail of sculpture by Aleijandinho, Ouro Preto

Lisboa was born in 1730, the son of a Portuguese architect and a Negro slave woman. As a young man he became famous for his religious sculptures of wood and stone. When he was about forty years old, he contracted the crippling disease of leprosy. Eventually his arms and legs were reduced to stumps and his face was so horribly disfigured that people turned and ran from him.

Not even the loss of his hands could stop Aleijadinho from working. A servant tied his tools to the stumps of Lisboa's arms so that he could continue to sculpture. During the time he was crippled, he fashioned out of stone twelve life-sized figures of the prophets.

28

The old church of San Bento, Rio de Janeiro

A modern church in Pampulha

30

They may still be seen in the mining town of Ouro Preto, and are visited every Easter by thousands of people.

The architecture of Brazil's colonial days is what is called "baroque." It is ornate, and the colonial buildings are decorated with many ornaments and statues. Many of these buildings are still being used today.

The modern buildings of Brazil are very different from the baroque ones. Today the architecture is plain, with little decoration. A great deal of glass and steel is used in construction, but the most widely used material of all is concrete. Since concrete can be poured into molds, buildings can be made in all kinds of shapes. Many of them are curved and sometimes look like huge bowls or saucers.

Coffee Galore

ALTHOUGH Brazil is the greatest coffee producer in the world, the coffee plant is not native to that country. It is said that the coffee tree originated in Ethiopia and was taken to the Middle East by Arab travelers. Many years before Brazil was discovered, coffee was a popular drink throughout Europe. Coffee plants were eventually brought to the West Indies and from there to South America.

The first Brazilian coffee plants were grown in the northern part of the country, but it was later found that the rich red earth of Minas Gerais, São Paulo, and Paraná yielded the best crops. As trade with North America grew and the United States developed into a nation of coffee drinkers, Brazilian coffee farmers began to plant millions of acres of coffee trees.

A coffee farm in Brazil is called a *fazenda* and is sometimes a small town in itself. The owner usually lives in a large house with

Picking coffee berries, or "cherries"

a tile roof made from the same red clay in which the coffee trees grow so well. Near the "big house" are smaller houses for the workers and their families. If the *fazenda* is a large and rich one, it probably has its own water system, telephone, electric lights, shops, school, church, and even its own small hospital.

A large *fazenda* may have four or five thousand acres of land, or even more. In addition to coffee, the owner may raise several hundred cattle, to furnish meat and milk, and fertilizer for his trees. He may also raise sugar cane, as the leaves make good fodder for his cattle. And he may grow other crops such as soy beans, which put back into the soil such needed chemicals as nitrogen.

Each working member of a coffee laborer's family is given about two thousand trees to care for. If a man and his wife and two grown children work, the family is thus responsible for eight thousand plants. The worker is also given enough land for his own vegetable garden, and a few chickens, pigs, and perhaps his own milk cow.

Most of Brazil lies south of the equator, and there the seasons are the opposite of those to its north. Spring comes from September to December, and that is when the coffee plants are in flower. The snowy-white blossoms have a heavy fragrance. After the flowers come the berries, which are about the size of a small marble. The ripe berries are a bright holly red and, like the flowers, are sweet-smelling. Inside each berry there are usually two little green beans, covered by a thin, parchment-like husk. These are the coffee beans which, when dried, roasted, and ground, can be brewed into the well-known steaming hot drink.

When the coffee berries are ripe they are picked and spread on sunny platforms where they are turned often with big wooden rakes so that they will dry evenly. Then they are washed in wooden troughs or sluices and are once more put in the sun. After they are

33

Fruit and flower of the coffee tree

again thoroughly dry they are put into sacks and taken to the husking machine. This machine separates the inside beans from their husk and the outside protective covering of the berry.

Again the beans are put into sacks and are ready for their trip to Santos, on the Atlantic Ocean about forty miles from São Paulo. In Santos is the Coffee Exchange, where brokers buy and sell the shipments of coffee which have arrived from the *fazendas*, sometimes by railroad, sometimes by truck, and often by mule cart.

Coffee beans vary in flavor, and even the beans from one tree may taste differently according to the weather of the particular

Drying coffee beans

year they were picked. Flavor is important to buyers, and many of the wholesalers have large, air-conditioned offices in Santos where they employ expert tasters. The tasters' job is to choose just the right blend of coffee beans for a particular brand of coffee.

A professional taster can tell one cup of coffee brew from another even after sipping hundreds of cups daily. His sense of taste is so acute that he can detect the slightest variation in flavor immediately. Coffee tasters must observe as strict training rules as athletes. They must never smoke, drink alcoholic beverages, or eat hot, spicy foods, else they may ruin their delicate sense of taste.

A coffee taster sits at a small, slowly turning table on which is a circle of tiny numbered cups of steaming black coffee. The taster only sips, then spits out the coffee into a basin, as swallowing the coffee would spoil his ability to taste properly. As he tastes, he chooses the best, second-best, and third-best blends.

Brazilians in general are great coffee drinkers. Everywhere one sees shops with long counters at which businessmen are taking a "coffee break," either in the morning or the afternoon. Along the sidewalks of cities and towns are cafés where people sit to drink tiny cups of thick, inky-black coffee — without cream, but with plenty of sugar. Some Brazilians drink dozens of these little cupfuls every day, and guests in business offices as well as in private homes are always offered a cup of coffee.

A Variety of Products

IN ADDITION to coffee, Brazilian farmers grow other important and valuable crops for their own use and for export to other countries. Cotton and rice are two of the largest crops each year. Two of the most important commercial crops are cacao (chocolate) and tobac-

Brazil nut tree in a jungle clearing

co. Oranges, bananas, pineapples, mangoes, and other tropical fruits are raised. Much of the *herva maté* tea that is grown in the south and southwestern areas is exported to Argentina and Uruguay.

The forests of Brazil are rich in trees bearing fruits and nuts valuable for their natural oils. Almost 865 million acres of Brazil's land are forested, and much of their timber is highly prized throughout the world.

Cattle-raising is important, and fine herds of Hereford and Black Angus cattle supply the country with excellent beef. Holstein and Jersey cows produce milk for cities and towns. The Brahman or zebu, a cow with humped shoulders, has been imported from its native India and is widely used because the Brazilian climate suits it so well.

Many valuable minerals and precious stones are mined in Brazil. Iron deposits are rich, and Brazil has about 23 per cent of all the iron in the world. Oil has been found in many sections of the country and is being produced. Coal is plentiful, but the quality is poor.

The carbonado or black diamond, used for tools, saws, and grinding devices, is found in Brazil. There are also gem diamonds, but the prized blue-white stones are rare. Most of the gem diamonds are yellow or sometimes pinkish. One of the world's largest diamonds, the "Vargas," was found in the diamond mines of Minas Gerais. Aquamarines, topazes, amethysts, and tourmalines are all found in Brazil.

Most Brazilians, even the men, wear rings set with one of the native stones, which are plentiful and quite inexpensive. Brazilians love jewelry. Even the little girls have their ears pierced and often wear tiny gold earrings set with a chip diamond or a stone of some other kind.

38

HESS — CUSHING

Loading cut rice onto an oxcart

Tapping a Brazilian rubber tree

The Rubber Boom—and Its End

SOME seventy or eighty years ago, all the world's rubber came from South America — most of it from the forests of the Amazon River Basin. Millions of dollars were made by the men who hired Indians to go into the jungles and gather rubber from the wild trees, although the Indians themselves were not paid much for their dangerous and unhealthy work.

At that time the seeds of the trees were jealously guarded by the rubber owners and the Brazilian government. Then, about 1876, Henry Wickham, an English coffee planter in the Amazon River region, got native Indians to collect about seventy thousand rubber seeds. He packed these between layers of banana leaves and put them into wicker baskets to be shipped overseas to England. When the seeds arrived, they were planted in beds at London's Kew Gardens. Almost three thousand of them grew into thriving plants.

The British were anxious to experiment with rubber plants in Britain's Far Eastern colonies, particularly in Ceylon, Malaya, and India. English plantation-owners in those countries believed that the climate and soil were right for rubber trees. They knew that if they could domesticate the rubber plants and grow them under cultivation they could produce more rubber for less money than the rubber barons of Brazil did.

Of the almost three thousand plants that grew successfully at Kew Gardens, about half were shipped to Ceylon. Almost all of them lived to produce the valuable "black gold," as rubber was called in those days. Finally, seeds and plants were cultivated in Malaya and sent on to India and Java. By 1922 the Far East was producing 93 per cent of the world's rubber, and the rubber ports of the Amazon River were ghost towns.

41

During World War II, as the Japanese captured more and more of the British possessions in the Far East, the Allies lost their vital source of rubber supply. They needed rubber for airplane, jeep, and truck tires as well as for other military supplies. Fortunately the manufacture of synthetic rubber was perfected during that time and raw rubber became less important.

The Ford Motor Company of Detroit, Michigan, did try to revive the Brazilian rubber industry, however, and spent millions of dollars in the Amazon region during the war years. The company called their plantation "Fordlandia," and its operation was kept a carefully guarded secret. The Ford experts tried to plant rubber as the British had done in the Far East, but Amazon jungle conditions and the difficulty of getting workers to stay on the job proved too much. Today "Fordlandia" is another of the rubber ghost towns.

In Brazil today rubber is still produced, but the synthetics have largely taken over the industry, and real rubber is used commercially in relatively small quantities. The loss of the profits from rubber is one of the reasons Brazil has concentrated on building up its industrial might — factories and steel mills, railroads and airports. Brazilians know that in the twentieth-century jet and space age a large country cannot live by the products of the land alone.

Some Cities of Brazil

Rio de Janeiro

WHETHER one arrives in Rio de Janeiro by airplane or by ship, probably the first things to catch his eye will be the famous Sugar

Air view of the harbor, Rio de Janeiro

43

Loaf Mountain, a tall granite hulk jutting out of Rio's Guanabara Bay, and the enormous statue of Christ standing atop an even higher peak called the "Hunchback." At night the statue of Christ is lighted and can be seen from many miles away by approaching visitors.

Rio, until 1960 the capital of Brazil, is a bustling modern city. Its harbor is said to have been discovered on New Year's Day, 1502, by Portuguese explorers. It was given its name, which means River of January, because the discoverers believed Guanabara Bay to be a river. Today the bay, dotted by many islands, is known as one of the most beautiful harbors in the world.

View of Rio de Janeiro

HESS — CUSHING

Just a few miles to the west of Rio's seacoast boundary is another boundary of green, heavily wooded mountains. As its population has increased in the past several years, the city has become very crowded. With the sea on one side and the mountains on the other, Rio has nowhere to go. Some of its smaller volcanic hills, or *morros*, have been flattened out to make room for more houses and roads.

The more than two million people who live in Rio call themselves "Cariocas," a nickname adopted from the Indian language. When the Portuguese founded the city, the Indians called it "carioca," meaning "the white man's house."

Rio is a very old city and many of its pale-pink colonial buildings still stand, but every day more modern, glistening-white apartment houses and glass-and-steel office buildings are being built.

The people are fond of flowers and fountains, and the parks and squares of Rio are planted with brilliantly colored tropical flowers. Fountains play night and day, and many of them are lighted after dark. The Botanical Gardens contain the largest collection of orchids in the world, besides many other plants and trees from all over the globe. The driveway to the gardens is lined by one hundred and thirty waving royal palm trees. The private park of the last emperor of Brazil is now public, also, and is a favorite of "Carioca" families for their Sunday walks.

Many of the sidewalks of Rio are especially colorful because they are made of small, colored tiles in bright mosaic patterns. The wear and tear on these sidewalks is considerable, and along the crowded streets of the business district the pedestrian must keep an eye out for breaks in the tile walks, lest he stub his toe.

Besides being noted for its many museums and parks, its opera house and cathedral, and its beautiful natural setting, Rio is probably best known for its beaches and its yearly, three-day carnival.

45

Botanical Gardens, Rio de Janeiro

The most famous beach of all is the Copacabana, with miles of pure white sand on the Atlantic Coast. The avenue that runs alongside it is a street of elegant white apartment houses and fashionable hotels and restaurants. From early in the morning until dark the beach is crowded, but bathers must be good swimmers because the undertow is usually strong and the surf rough.

46

Mosaic sidewalks, Rio de Janeiro

47

STEVENS — CUSHING

Copacabana Beach, Rio de Janeiro

48

Like all big cities, Rio has its slums of poor and uneducated people. Their shacks, built along narrow, winding streets, dot many of the hillsides and are often just next door to the homes of the wealthy. Little by little the government is tearing down these slums, called *favelas*, and is building clean modern houses.

Almost all the "Cariocas" of Portuguese descent are of the Roman Catholic faith, but many of the people of African ancestry still practice and believe in the pagan rites of "Candoble," or "Macumba." These primitive practices are closely related to the voodoo rites of the island of Haiti.

During Macumba ceremonies, offerings are made to ancient African gods, such as First God, Thunder God, War God, and the goddesses of the waters and fertility. Food and drink are offered to the gods and goddesses while women dancers dressed in brightly colored costumes perform ritual dances. The dancing is accompanied by the strange Macumba music, a mixture of African drumbeats and Latin rhythms, and singing and chanting by the spectators. When the ceremonies finally reach an end, the dancers and musicians are all but exhausted. It seems strange that in a modern city this pagan worship should still go on, but it is found today not only in Rio but in other cities of Brazil.

São Paulo

SÃO PAULO, south of Rio and forty miles inland from the port of Santos, is the fastest-growing city in the world today, and is already larger than Rio. It is the heart of industrial Brazil and the gateway to the vast coffee-growing country.

Very little of the old has been preserved in São Paulo. Narrow streets have been widened to make way for heavy traffic; there are many skyscraper office buildings and hotels, and new ones are being completed each month. The "Paulistas," as the citizens of São Paulo are called, are generally more wealthy than most of their countrymen, and many of their homes are luxurious, with beautiful gardens and swimming pools. "Paulista" housewives make their work easier with the help of washing machines, refrigerators, vacuum cleaners, and other household gadgets.

A short drive from the center of São Paulo is the world-famous Butantan Snake Farm and Museum. Here scientists extract venom from poisonous snakes and manufacture the antivenom serum that saves thousands of lives each year. Butantan was the first such research center in the world.

The snakes live in little igloo-shaped houses of red clay, built in deep pits and shaded by jacaranda and other tropical trees. The reptiles are free to wander in and out of their houses, or if they like they may climb one of the trees and hang from its branches.

To extract venom from a poisonous snake, an attendant pins it down with a strong forked stick. Then he quickly grasps the snake just behind its head. Holding a glass container under its open mouth, he catches the venom as it falls in drops from the fangs. One drop of venom from a rattlesnake is capable of killing ten men.

People who live in the country and jungles all over South America catch snakes and send them in boxes to the snake farm. In return, the farm sends serum manufactured from the venom — one type of serum for each type of poisonous snake common to the district and one serum effective against all poisonous snake bites, to be used when a person is uncertain what kind of snake bit him. Whenever anyone is bitten by a poisonous snake he hurries to the nearest farmhouse to get an injection of serum.

At Butantan there are also non-poisonous snakes. Sometimes farmers ask to have these reptiles on their farms because they help kill insects and rats and mice.

exotic tropical birds and flowers. Many of the statues of the saints wear necklaces of colored beads. While many of Salvador's churches are highly decorated, this is the most lavish of all.

In one of the smaller churches, the Chapel of Graca, is a crudely carved wooden statue of the Virgin. There is a romantic story connected with this old statue. According to the legend, one of the early Portuguese settlers, Diego Alves Correira, was rescued by an Indian princess as the men of her tribe were about to kill him. Later she married the white man and was baptized a Christian. She dreamed that divers could find a statue of the Virgin in a sunken ship that lay at the bottom of the harbor. The statue in the Chapel of Graca is said to be the one about which the princess dreamed. The people of Salvador are very fond of this Virgin and have given her a pure gold crown and a robe of sky-blue cloth.

Recife

RECIFE, the capital of the northeastern state of Pernambuco, is the most easterly port of South America. Its name is the Portuguese word for "reef," because of the coral reefs around its harbor. Many people call Recife the "Venice of Brazil" because the city, partly on an island, is crossed by canals and connected by bridges.

Early in the seventeenth century the Dutch West India Company formed a colony in Pernambuco and managed to defend it against the Portuguese for ten years. Finally, in 1654, the Dutch gave in, and Pernambuco and the city of Recife became a part of Portuguese Brazil. Today, very few of the Dutch colonial buildings remain.

Until recent years, about half of Recife consisted of terrible slums, called *mucambos*, built on low, swampy ground. Here the long, narrow houses were usually made of thin bamboo poles stuck

55

Inner harbor, Recife

together with mud and adobe, though sometimes they were made of wood, tin, or plaster. The roofs were thatched, and the interiors were partitioned into rooms with dirt floors and no ceilings. Disease and poverty in the *mucambos* caused many deaths each year. Gradually the low land has been filled in, however; modern houses have been built and the *mucambos* destroyed. Today Recife is a clean, attractive city and a thriving seaport.

56

There are many interesting old churches in Recife — several of them Dutch churches which still stand. Many of the seventeenth-century houses with their pink stucco walls, latticed balconies, and heavy carved doors remind one of Portugal. Just a few minutes drive from the mainland part of the city is the quaint old town of Olinda, famous for its magnificent beach.

Oil and wax from varieties of the palm tree are shipped from Recife, as are sugar and cotton.

Seminary, Olinda

Belém

ON THE Pará River, ninety miles from the Atlantic Ocean, is another port city named Belém, which means Bethlehem. It is a jumping-off spot for travelers to the interior of the Amazon jungle. The climate of the city is hot and sticky, but frequent rain showers help to cool the streets and keep the air fresh. In the main square, palm trees shade the walks and it is not uncommon to see a man with a pet monkey which may perform tricks for passers-by.

Shopping for alligator skins, Belém

For a glimpse of what the wild Amazon country is like, there is a public park, the Bosque. This is a relatively untouched area and along its paths one may get the feel of the dark, silent jungle — but without the fear of dangerous snakes or other jungle hazards. In the middle of the Bosque is a deep pond, and nearby is a dark cave which can be explored by those who do not mind bats flying within inches of their heads.

There is a zoo in Belém. Here cages of wild animals such as South American leopards and coatis, and aviaries of parrots, parakeets, and macaws are placed in a lush, tropical setting of flowering trees and shrubs.

In the market place one may buy alligator skins as long as a man is tall, or tiny stuffed alligators. Brightly colored, hand-painted gourds are strung up at the sides of the stalls, and clay pots of all sizes and shapes are for sale. Leopard and jaguar skins are also displayed, together with hand-woven baskets, wood carvings, and tropical fruit and tobacco. The dark-skinned women merchants, many of them carrying their wares in baskets on their heads, are dressed in gay cotton prints, and the market is a riot of color.

Manaus

A FOUR-DAY trip by river steamer up the Amazon from the Atlantic Ocean will bring a person to Manaus. There are no roads leading to the city, and the only means of transportation to it is by air or boat.

Manaus is hilly, and from the hilltops can be seen the junction of the Amazon and the Rio Negro or Black River, which is indeed inky black. At the city docks are tied the boats which carry loads of Brazil nuts, lumber, rubber, and medicinal herbs and plants down the river to Belém, from where they are shipped to the ports

HESS — CUSHING

Opera House, Manaus

60

of the world. Alongside the larger boats are tied the long dugout canoes of the Indian rubber-gatherers and farmers who have journeyed to the city for a day's shopping or to bring their products to sell in the public market.

Although it is truly a jungle city, Manaus has many modern buildings such as a luxury hotel, an air-conditioned theater, and an apartment-house skyscraper. Probably the most famous of all its buildings is the Opera House, built in 1896 when fortunes were being made from rubber. The building's huge dome of green, yellow, blue, and red French tiles sparkles in the tropical sun and can be seen from all over the city.

What is probably one of the tiniest churches in the world was built in Manaus by a poor worker. It is called *Igreja do Pobre Diabo*, or "Church of the Poor Worker." Scarcely more than a dozen people can squeeze into the miniature building, which is only twelve feet wide and fifteen feet long.

Brazil Moves West

EVER SINCE 1798 the Brazilian people had dreamed of opening up their western frontier and moving the capital of their country from Rio de Janeiro, on the seacoast, to the center of Brazil. When the Republic of Brazil was founded in 1889, the new constitution declared that about 9,000 square miles should be set aside for a future capital. Shortly after that, a famous Brazilian leader, Luis Cruls, chose a group of astronomers, doctors, engineers, and botanists to go with him to explore the land to the west.

After several months, and many hundreds of miles of travel on horseback and on foot over the mountains and through jungles and desert, the explorers returned to Rio de Janeiro. They told the government that they considered the Central Plateau, about in the center of the country, a perfect spot for the new capital. On the plateau, about 3,000 feet above sea level, they had discovered rich, rolling farmland, where cattle and sheep could easily be raised, also. Moreover they had found lakes and rivers where dams could be built to provide water power. Perhaps most important of all, they had discovered springs of safe drinking water, and a healthier climate than the humid heat of Rio.

But even though the explorers had found what seemed to be an ideal place for the new capital, the government remained in Rio. In those days there were no bulldozers to dig up the forest trees, no tractors and roadscrapers to build the roads, no big trucks, jeeps, or airplanes to carry supplies from Rio and São Paulo. Besides, the Brazilians had come to love their beautiful capital of Rio de Janeiro with its miles of white beaches and its warm, sunny climate. The people did not want to move.

Finally, in 1956, when Kubitschek became President of Brazil, he promised that the new capital of Brasilia would be built and ready to be occupied by April, 1960.

Before a new city could be built in the wilderness, however, there must be a plan. The Brazilian government held a competition for the best city plan. The winner was Lucio Costa, and the architect chosen to design the buildings was the world-famous Oscar Niemeyer, of Rio.

The city is laid out like a big airplane. On its wings are built houses, apartment buildings, parks, and public gardens. The body of the airplane contains the radio and television towers, the sports fields, and the plaza, or square. On the propellers is a large shopping center. The tail of the airplane is for the government buildings and the cathedral. In his city plan Costa also included areas

A native child in a dugout, Amazon River valley

BRAZILIAN GOVERNMENT TRADE BUREAU

Presidential Palace, Brasilia

64

for a president's palace, an artificial lake large enough for fishing and sailing, a golf course, a jet airport, hospitals, schools, churches, and hotels.

The site chosen for Brasilia was a vast stretch of thick pine forest. Before buildings could be raised, the land had to be cleared of trees, and roads had to be built from the coast so that bulldozers and tractors, and cement, steel, and other building materials could be brought in. Although Brasilia itself is on a cool plateau, the roads had to run through steamy jungles full of poisonous snakes and savage animals, and over hot deserts where the sun beat down on the workers all day long. Road building in such an area is a difficult task.

Thousands of people came from all over Brazil and from Europe and North America to help build the new roads and the city. Day and night one could hear the chugging of the tractors and the crashing of the tall trees as the bulldozers uprooted them. Once enough land had been cleared at the site of the city, a landing field was made so that airplanes could bring in food and supplies quickly.

For a long time the city looked like a huge sea of red, sticky mud. Everyone wore khaki pants, thick, heavy boots, and wide-brimmed straw hats as protection against the sun. For a time the workers had to live in tents and sleep in hammocks. After a few months, workmen were at least able to install electric power lines, telephone lines, and sewers, however.

After a while a temporary town of small shacks for the workers sprang up, which people called "Freetown." It looked like a television or movie version of a "Wild West" town, with its muddy main street lined on each side by one-story buildings containing banks, restaurants, movie theaters, shops, and cafés.

65

BRAZILIAN GOVERNMENT TRADE BUREAU

Houses of Congress, Brasilia

As the buildings designed by Niemeyer began to take shape, people stared in amazement. These were not like any buildings they had ever seen before. Brasilia is a city of the twentieth century, and Niemeyer has used a modern style of architecture for it. The president's palace, called the Palace of Dawn, is a long, low building, its sides almost all glass and its roof supported by concrete pillars shaped like big, thin triangles. The Chamber of Deputies, where Congress meets, looks from the outside like a big, shallow soup bowl of gray concrete. When Brazilians attend services in the new cathedral, they will sit underground in a basement room. The outside of the glass-and-cement cathedral resembles a morning-glory flower turned upside down.

The apartment buildings are tall and white. They have little balconies upon which people can sit to enjoy the cool breezes that blow every evening. In the residential parts of the city there will be a chapel every other block, for the Brazilians are devout churchgoers.

The city's children will be especially guarded against traffic, as they can use the footbridges which will be built over busy streets, or the sidewalks which will run underneath elevated roads.

The city was ready on schedule and was dedicated on April 21, 1960. Today the roads from the north, south, and east are busy with traffic to Brasilia. Already more than ten thousand people are living in the new capital, but building will go on for many years. There is still much work to be done.

Carnival

ALL YEAR LONG as the "Cariocas" of Rio de Janeiro work and go to school, they look forward to one three-day holiday — Carnival.

Men, women, and children save their *cruzeiros* (the Brazilian money) to buy a costume for this event. Although Carnival is celebrated throughout Latin America, no other is as exciting as that of Rio. People come from all over the world to see and take part in it.

Carnival is a time for dancing in the streets, parades, fancy dress balls, and general gaiety. It starts on the Saturday before Ash Wednesday, the beginning of the Christian Lenten season.

There are many Carnival clubs and teams which compete to win prizes for the best dancing, the best songs and music composed especially for the Carnival, the best costumes, and the most beautiful and original floats. Sometimes the costumes for Carnival are made of costly silks and satins, and represent lords and ladies of the empire days, and sometimes the costumes are only meant to be funny.

As the day for Carnival draws near, everyone in Rio is excited. Millions of packages of confetti are sold, and so are "serpentines," long, thin strips of colored paper rolled into tight, round disks. When a person holds one end of the paper and throws the disk, it unravels into a long streamer. Almost everyone buys a mask. Some of the masks are small and cover only the nose and eyes, but others may be animal faces or may represent the face of a famous person. Sometimes the masks are huge, grotesque heads made of papier-mâché.

A few days before Carnival, every household in Rio is busy putting last-minute touches to costumes and planning parties and dances. Children and grownups alike buy horns and other noise-makers. Carnival clubs hold final rehearsals in the hope that their entries will win the prizes. Preparations are all very secret. Everyone wants to surprise everyone else. Keeping people guessing is half the fun.

Children, dressed for Carnival party

In Rio the festivities open at noon on Saturday. Until the following Wednesday everything stops for the three-day holiday.

On Sunday night, large groups known as the "samba schools" parade in costume. They have their own bands and have made up songs and music which they play for the judges. On Monday night the "ranchos," which are similar but smaller groups, parade. The music of the "ranchos" is sadder and slower than the gay rhythms of the "samba schools." Tuesday, the last night of Carnival, is the most exciting and colorful of all. It is then that the huge floats and decorated automobiles drive slowly through the city in a parade that seems endless.

By Wednesday morning, Carnival is over and the streets are almost deserted except for the street cleaners, who are busy gathering up the tons of confetti and the miles of paper serpentines. Most "Cariocas" are fast asleep, exhausted from the holiday but already dreaming of their plans for next year's Carnival.

Religious and National Holidays

ON A PENINSULA in the old city of Salvador there is a little eighteenth-century church named the Church of Our Lord of Bomfim (Bomfim means Good End). On Fridays and Sundays, people make pilgrimages to this church, offering special gifts to the saints. On the Feast of the Epiphany there is a great procession to the Church of Our Lord of Bomfim. Some of the people come in boats and canoes decorated with flowers.

Since many people of Salvador are fishermen or otherwise earn their living from the sea, they have a yearly procession to honor

Fisherman, mending net

71

Statue of Tiradentes, Sao Paulo

Our Lord of Seafarers. A statue of the saint is taken from one of the churches on the Salvador waterfront and put aboard a boat, which has a winged guardian angel as a figurehead. Sailors, dressed in blue and white and rowing in unison with bright blue oars, take the statue to another church on the waterfront and then return it to its starting point. The boat carrying Our Lord of Seafarers is followed by an escort of boats and canoes. When the statue is returned to its own church it is greeted by crowds of people and by priests in beautiful robes. It is then taken inside, where it will stay until the next year, when the ceremony will be repeated.

To celebrate the birthdays of St. John the Baptist and St. Peter and St. Paul, all of which occur at the end of June, people of the central sections of Brazil hold fancy dress balls somewhat like country barn dances. They dress in funny "hillbilly" costumes and dance folk dances.

Other religious holidays include Ash Wednesday, Good Friday, Assumption of the Blessed Virgin on August 15, All Souls Day on November 2, Immaculate Conception on December 8, and Christmas Day.

Brazilians celebrate their national independence on September 7 and the Proclamation of the Republic on November 15. May 1 is Brazilian Labor Day, and April 21 is a national holiday in honor of Tiradentes, a young Brazilian patriot who was executed during colonial days for conspiring against the government. Tiradentes, or "Tooth Puller," was so called because he was a dentist. The revolt of Tiradentes and his followers started in Ouro Preto in 1789, but was put down by the government, and the leader was caught and hanged. His memory is honored by his countrymen because he was the first Brazilian to lead a movement for independence.

A Glimpse into a Wilderness

IT IS hard to believe that, in the twentieth-century jet age, there should remain mysterious, unexplored regions of the world. There are such places, however, and one of the most intriguing is the western state of Mato Grosso, in Brazil.

Almost since the time when the white men first came to Brazil, the mysterious lands of Mato Grosso have excited explorers. During the nineteenth century many expeditions attempted to penetrate the interior of this wild tropical state. Some explorers returned with valuable scientific information about the animals, the Indians, and the land and waterways of Mato Grosso. But many others died, and still others came home seriously ill of fever and tropical diseases. Some explorers disappeared and were never heard of again. They may have been killed by Indian tribes such as the warlike Chavantes, who even today are not very friendly to white men.

It is little wonder that pioneers did not rush to make settlements in this wild region. There are fair-sized towns in the southern part of Mato Grosso — towns such as the state capital, Cuiabá, a cattle-raising center, and Corumbá, a steel town and a center for the valuable manganese mining industry. But north of Cuiabá there is little more than wilderness, stretching up through the state of Pará to the Amazon River.

What is this no man's land really like?

Across the Araguaia River, which forms the eastern boundary of Mato Grosso, is the *cerrado*, a dry plain dotted with gnarled, stubby trees and plants. There is little grass on the *cerrado*, and the region is dry and dusty. The hot sun beats down for months on end and not much rain falls.

74

An Indian of the Mato Grosso

A trip through the *cerrado* can be uncomfortable. Tiny stinging flies, bees, and wasps are all too eager to take a nip from an explorer. They like the salty taste of human perspiration.

Ants of many varieties abound in Mato Grosso. Among others there are leafcutter ants, red ants, and white ants which build hills so hard that a grown man can easily sit on one without breaking it. But on the *cerrado*, also, are two species of ant bear. The so-called "great anteater" is over eight feet long, including its tail, and it weighs about ninety pounds. It has powerful claws which can tear apart the white ant's sturdy hill, and it has a long, sticky tongue with which it laps up ants almost faster than the eye can see. The great anteater and its slightly smaller cousin are said to be so powerful that even the jaguar is no match for them.

To the north, the *cerrado* gives way to real jungle growth. Tall trees of more than a hundred feet must be cut down and thick undergrowth cleared away before a campsite can be made. If an airplane is to land, a clearing must first be made in the dense jungle.

Because it would be impossible to carry enough food for a lengthy expedition, guides hunt and fish to eke out the supplies. Armadillo, lizard, and tortoise meat are common foods.

Crossing the territory of the Chavante Indians in this area is still dangerous although the Brazilian government has, to some degree, succeeded in making friends with these ferocious savages. They are very good shots with bows and arrows, and sometimes leave arrows as warnings along the paths of exploring expeditions.

The Chavante Indians live in round mud huts roofed with palm leaves and placed in a semicircle. They build their villages near streams so that fresh water is always available. In their gardens they raise maize — or corn — cotton, and gourds. Often when they

76

hunt they light fires to attract wild animals and trap them. Then the hunters slaughter the animals with their arrows and spears.

Many of the Xingu River tribes in Mato Grosso are friendly to white men. The Kalapalo of the Karaiba tribe are one such group. They are of medium height and fairly stocky. The men cut their thick black hair in a bob, leaving a small shaven spot on the top of their heads. They do not shave their beards, but pluck them instead. The women cut their hair in short bangs over their foreheads, but otherwise wear it long. For scissors the Kalapalo use the razor-sharp teeth of the piranha, a particularly dangerous fish.

The Kalapalo Indians wear no clothes at all, but stain their skin a deep tobacco brown with plant juices and oils which help protect them against insect bites. The Indians are very clean and bathe several times a day.

The houses of the Kalapalo are oval-shaped huts, thatched with grass and palm leaves. About thirty people, usually a family group, live in each hut. They sleep in hammocks arranged in a fanlike position. During the winter months, when it is damp and chilly, a small fire is kept going all night and is tended throughout the dark hours by the head woman of the house.

Because disease is so common and because many babies are born weak and sickly, the Kalapalo and other Xingu tribes kill the infants who are not likely to grow to be adults. In this way they hope to keep their tribe strong.

There are other tribes of Indians living in the Mato Grosso, some friendly, others hostile. The Brazilian Department of Indian Affairs tries to protect them from unscrupulous white men, and persons wishing to travel into the interior of the Mato Grosso must secure a government permit.

An Indian girl in reservation school

For almost twenty years a small construction team has been trying to build a road from Santarém on the Amazon River in the state of Pará to Chavantina, in the center of Mato Grosso. The work will probably not be completed for many more years. It goes slowly because of the jungle, the climate, and the difficulty of keeping supplies moving. Many workers will not stay on the job, moreover, for the work is discouraging.

Although there are quantities of unused land and probably new riches to be found in Mato Grosso, it is doubtful that many settlers will move into the state for years to come. Until roads and airports are built, only the most adventurous will dare the rigors and dangers of the region. And roads and airports will probably be slow to come, because Brazil still has so much other unoccupied land that is more suitable for settlers. These other lands will be opened up first by the pioneers of Brazil.

Index

Aircraft, use of, in interior, 1, 2, 42, 62, 65, 76, 79

Aleijadinho, (Antonio Francisco Lisboa), 27, 28

Amazon Basin, 3, 18, 41, 42, 58, 59

Amazon River, 41, 59, 74, 78

Andrada e Silva, José Bonifácio de, 11

Animals, wild, 1, 59, 65, 74, 76, 77

Anteater, 76

Ants. *See* Insects

Araguaia River, 74

Architecture, 23, 31, 45, 49, 51, 53, 57, 61, 62, 65, 67

Argentina, 6, 38

Art, 27, 28, 44, 53, 55

Atlantic Ocean, 3, 34, 58, 59

Bahia, 7, 9, 15, 51

Beaches, 45, 46, 57, 62

Belém, 58, 59

Belo Horizonte, 51

Black River, 59

Bombachas, 23

Bosque, the, 59

Botanical Gardens, in Rio de Janeiro, 45

Brasilia, new capital, 13, 62, 65, 67

Brazil, United States of:
  boundaries of, 3, 6
  colonization of, by Portuguese, 9
  discovery of, by Portuguese, 1, 7
  geography of, 1, 3, 6
  origin of name, 7, 9
  people of, 15, 18, 49, 53, 77
  size of, 3

Brazilwood, 9

Butantan, 50, 51

Caboclos, 18

Cabral, Pedro Alvares, 7, 9

Cacao bean (chocolate), 36, 53

"Candoble." *See* Rituals, primitive

"Cariocas," 45, 49, 67, 70

Carnival, 45, 67, 68, 70

Cattle raising, 6, 23, 25, 33, 38, 51, 62, 74

Ceremonies, African, 49

Cerrado plain, 74, 76

Chapel of Grace, legend of, 55

Chavantina, 78

Christ, statue of, 44

Churches, 18, 53, 55, 57, 61, 65, 67, 70, 73

Climate, 3, 23, 58, 62, 65, 74

Coffee industry:
  Coffee Exchange, 34
  export of, 13, 23, 31, 34
  plantations, 31, 33
  tasters, professional, 36

Columbus, Christopher, 6

Copacabana Beach, 46

Correira, Diego Alves, 55

Cortes, the, 11

Corumbá, 74

Costa, Lucio, 62

Cowboys. *See* Gaucho

Crops, important, 18, 23, 25, 31, 33, 36, 38, 53, 57, 59

Cruls, Luis, 61

Cruzeiro (Brazilian money), 68

Cuiabá, 74

Diamonds, 38, 51

Dictatorship, 13

Diseases, tropical, 1, 74

Dutch West India Company, 55

Equator, 3

Expansion, westward, 1, 2, 3, 13, 25, 61, 62, 65, 79

Export products, 13, 31, 34, 36, 38, 53, 57, 59

Family life, 27

Farmers, Japanese, 18

Favelas, see slums

Fazenda, (coffee farm), 31, 33, 34

81

Fishing industry. *See* Industry
Fonseca, General Deodoro da, 13
Food and diet, 23, 25, 36, 38, 53, 76, 77
Ford Motor Company, 42
"Fordlandia," 42
Forests, 1, 3, 6, 38, 41, 65
Frontier, western, development of, 13, 61, 62, 65, 79

Gaucho, the, 6, 18, 23, 25
Goulart, Joao, 15
Government, forms of, 3, 9, 11, 13, 15, 18
Grasslands *(campos)*, 6
Great Escarpment, the, 3
Guanabara Bay, 44
Guarnieri, Carmargo, (composer), 27

Herva maté, see Tea, maté
Holidays, national, 68, 70, 73
Holidays, religious, 70, 73
Houses, types of, 21, 23, 31, 33, 45, 46, 49, 50, 53, 55, 56, 57, 61, 62, 65, 67, 76, 77

Iguassu Falls, 6
Immigration, 11, 18
India, 7, 41
Indian Affairs, Brazilian Dept. of, 77
Indians, of Brazil:
    Chavantes, 74, 76, 77
    Kalapalo (Karaiba tribe), 77
    Tupi-Guarani, 15
    Xingu, 77
Industry, 6, 10, 13, 15, 18, 21, 23, 25, 31, 33, 34, 36, 38, 41, 42, 49, 50, 51, 53, 57, 59, 61, 62, 65, 67, 74
Inhabitants, original, 7, 15
Insects, 1, 76

Jangadas, 18
John VI, King of Portugal, 9
Jungle, 1, 3, 41, 42, 50, 58, 59, 61, 65, 74, 76, 78

Kubitschek, Juscelino, 3, 13, 62

Languages, 18, 45
Library of Congress, Washington, D. C., 27

"Macumba." *See* Rituals, primitive
Manaus, 59, 61
Manganese, 74
Maria II, 11
Mato Grosso, 3, 74, 76, 77, 78, 79
Medicine, first school of, 9
Miguel, Dom, 11
Minas Gerais, 25, 31, 38, 51
Minerals, 38, 51, 53, 74
Mining. *See* Industry
Morros (volcanic hills), 45
Mucambos, see slums
Music and dance, 27, 49, 68, 70, 73

Napoleon, 9
Niemeyer, Oscar, 62, 67
Nigeria, West Africa, 18
Nuts, Brazil, 18, 38, 59

Occupations. *See* Industry
Olinda, 57
Opera House, in Manaus, 61
Orchids, 6, 45
Ouro Preto, 31, 51, 73

Palace of Dawn, 67
Pará, 58, 74, 78
Paraguay, 6, 25
Paraná, 31
"Paulistas," 50
Paulo Afonso Falls, 6
Pedro I, 9, 11
Pedro II, 11, 13
Penedo, 6
Pernambuco, 55
Philip II, King of Spain, 9
Piranha fish, 77
Portinari, Candido, artist, 27

Quadros, Senhor Janio, 15

Recife, capital of Pernambuco, 6, 55, 56, 57

Religions, 15, 18, 49
Rio de Janeiro:
  capital, former, 44, 61
  Carnival in, 45, 67, 68, 70
  houses of, 45, 46, 49
  mentioned, 9, 42, 44, 45, 49, 51, 53,
    61, 62, 67, 68, 70
  people of, 45, 49
  sidewalks, mosaic, 45
Rio Negro River, 59
Rituals, primitive, 49
Rubber industry, 41, 42, 59, 61

Salvador, 3, 6, 7, 51, 53, 55, 70, 73
Santarém, 78
Santos, 9, 34, 36
Sao Francisco River, 6
Sao Paulo, 15, 31, 34, 49, 50, 62
Serum, snake, 50, 51
Sheep raising, 62
Slavery, 11, 15, 18, 28, 53
Slums, 49, 55, 56
Snake farm, Butantan, 50
Snakes, 1, 50, 59, 65
Sousa, Martin Affonso de, 9

Spain, 6, 9, 11, 13, 27
Steel, 74
Sugar Loaf Mountain, 44
Swamps, 1, 55

Tea, maté, 23, 25, 38
Terra da Vera Cruz, 7
Tiradentes, revolt of, 73
Tobacco, 36, 53
Trade, open, 9
Tropical Zone, 3

United States of America, 3, 11
Uruguay, 3, 38

Vargas, Senhor Getulio, 13
"Venice of Brazil," (Recife), 55
Villa-Lobos, Heitor, (composer), 27

Warfare, between Indians and colonists,
  15
Wickham, Henry, 41
Women, status of, 27
World War II, 42

FIRST BOOKS
Complete Check List

Series No.	Quantity	TITLE / Author	Listings	Grade Reading Level
68		Atlas C S Hammond & Co	A sl L	3-4
22		Africa Hughes	A sl L CS	4-7
140		Air Knight	A sl L	4 up
1		Airplanes Bendick	A sl L C CS	3-6
76		American History Commager	A sl L C CS	4 up
11		The American Revolution Morris	A sl L C CS	5 up
158		Ancient Bible Lands Robinson	New Publication	
134		Ancient Egypt Robinson	A L	4 up
110		Ancient Greece Robinson	A L	4 up
150		Ancient Mesopotamia and Persia Robinson	A L	4 up
99		Ancient Rome Robinson	A L	4 up
73		The Antarctic Icenhower	A L C	4-7
77		Archaeology Kubie	A sl L C CS	4 up
135		Architecture Moore	A sl L	4 up
104		Astronomy Grey	A L	4, up
107		Australia Kaula	L	4-7
5		Automobiles Bendick	A sl L C CS	3-5
44		The Ballet Streatfeild	A sl L CS	4-7
148		Barbarian Invaders Sobol	A	5 up
14		Baseball Brewster	A sl L C CS	3-5
94		Basketball Schiffer	A sl L C	4-8
4		Bees Tibbets	A L C CS	3-6
98		Bells Fletcher	L CS	2-4
18		Birds Williamson	A sl L C	3-6
2		Boats Gossett	A L CS	2-4
101		Boys' Cooking Beim	A sl L C CS	4 up
149		Brazil Sheppard	A	4 up
43		Bridges Peet	A L C CS	3-7
6		Bugs Williamson	A sl L C CS H	3-5
153		California Gold Rush Havighurst	A L	4-7
65		Canada C & M Lineaweaver	A L C	4-6
139		Cartoons for Kids Fenner		2-5
111		Cats Taber	A sl L C	3-6
54		Caves E Hamilton	A sl L C	4-6
45		Chess Leeming	A sl L C CS H	5 up
173		The China Clippers Rich	New Publication	
146		Christmas Joy Wilson	A L	1-3
105		Civil War Land Battles Dupuy	A sl L C	5 up
137		Civil War Naval Actions Dupuy	A sl L	5 up
29		Codes and Ciphers S & B Epstein	A sl L C CS H	3-5
95		Color Paschel	A L C CS	5 up
157		Comunist China Kinmond	New Publication	
108		The Congo McDonnell	L	3-6
9		Congress Coy	A sl L C H	5 up
47		Conservation F C Smith	A sl L C CS	4-7
85		The Constitution Morris	A sl L C CS	5 up
40		Cotton Rogers	A L C CS	4-6
13		Cowboys Brewster	A sl L C	4 up
10		Dogs Taber	A L C CS	3-5
39		Dolls H Hoke	A sl L C CS	1-3
88		Drawing Slobodkin	A sl L C	6 up
96		The Early Settlers Rich	A sl L C	4-6
81		The Earth Sevrey	A L C	5 up
42		Electricity S & B Epstein	A sl L C CS	4-8
83		England Streatfeild	A L C CS	4-7
26		Eskimos Brewster	A sl L C CS	3-5
79		Fairy Tales Abell		3 up
25		Festivals Reck	A L C	3-6
21		Firemen Brewster	A L	3-5
69		Food Scheib	A L C CS	3-5
87		Football Schiffer	A sl L C	3 up
92		France Gottlieb	A sl L C	4-7
61		Gardening Kirkus	A sl L C	4-6
122		Ghana Lobsenz	A sl L	4-7
155		Glaciers Marcus	A L	4 up
60		Glass S & B Epstein	A L C CS	3-5
48		Hawaii S & B Epstein	A L C CS	4-6
62		Holidays Burnett	A L C	3-5
8		Horses McMeekin	A sl L C CS	5 up
129		How to Fix It Bendick-Berk	A sl L	3 up
143		Human Senses Liberty	A sl L	4 up
66		India Hahn	L C CS	4-7
103		The Indian Wars Morris	A	4 up
15		Indians (American) Brewster	A L C CS	2-6
41		Israel Kubie	A sl L C CS	4-7
89		Italy S & B Epstein	A sl L C CS	4-7
30		Japan Mears	A L C CS	4-7
58		Jazz Hughes	A L C CS H	7 up
19		Jokes Chrystie	A L C CS	3-6
130		Kings Newton	L	3-6
172		Language & How To Use It Applegate	New Publication	
159		Legendary Beings Jacobson	New Publication	
74		Letter Writing Jacobson	A L C CS	4-6
160		Light Harrison	New Publication	
152		Machines Buehr	A	3-6
46		Magic Stoddard	A sl L C CS	3-5
75		Mammals Williamson	A sl L C CS H	4 up
90		Maps and Globes S & B Epstein	A sl L C CS	4-6
125		Measurement S & B Epstein	L	4-6
102		Medieval Man Sobol	A sl L	4 up
123		The Mediterranean Gottlieb	A L	4-7
63		Mexico S & B Epstein	A L C H	4-7
35		Microbes Lewis	A sl L C CS H	4 up
116		Mining Markun	A sl L	3-6
51		Music Norman	A sl L C CS	3-6
128		Mythical Beasts Jacobson	A L	3-5
67		Mythology Elgin	A sl L CS	4 up
113		National Monuments Lobsenz	A L	3 up
115		National Parks Lobsenz	A L	3 up
27		Negroes Hughes	A sl L C CS	4 up
154		Netherlands Cohn	A	4 up
12		New England Rich	A L CS H	4-6
119		New World Explorers Rich	A L	4-6
131		New Zealand Kaula	A	4 up
72		Norse Legends Elgin	L	4-6
16		Nurses Elting	A sl L C CS	3-5
133		Ocean Epstein	A L	4 up
109		The Oregon Trail Havighurst	A L C	3-7
118		Paintings Moore	A sl L C	4 up
151		Pakistan Bothwell	A L	4 up
84		The Panama Canal Markun	A sl L C CS	4 up
50		Photography J Hoke	A sl L C CS H	5 up
142		Physical Fitness Walsh	A L	4 up
97		Pioneers Havighurst		4-8
38		Plants Dickinson	C CS	4 up
37		Poetry Peterson	A sl L C CS	3-6
53		Prehistoric Animals Dickinson	A sl L C CS	4-7
28		Presidents Coy	A L CS	4-6
64		Printing S & B Epstein	A sl L C CS H	5 up
114		Public Libraries Graham	L	2-4
24		Puppets Jagendorf	A L C	3-5
49		Rhythms Hughes	A sl L C CS	2-4
55		Roads Bothwell	A sl L C CS	3-5
136		Sailing M Lineaweaver	L C CS	8 up
31		Science Experiments Wyler	A sl L C	4-6

57	Sea Shells	Cavanna	A		L	C			3-6
100	Ships	Bendick	A		L	C	CS		3-6
23	Snakes	J Hoke	A	sl	L	C	CS	H	3 up
124	Sound	Knight	A	sl	L				4 up
141	South America	Carter	A		L				4 up
91	The Soviet Union	Snyder	A	sl	L	C	CS		5-8
34	Space Travel	Bendick	A	sl	L	C	CS		4-7
20	Stage Costume	Berk	A	sl	L	C	CS	H	5 up
171	Stone Age Man	Dickinson	New Publication						
7	Stones	Cormack	A	sl	L	C	CS	H	4 up
36	Submarines	Icenhower	A	sl	L	C	CS	H	4 up
56	Supermarkets	Bendick	A	sl	L	C	CS		1-4
86	The Supreme Court	Coy	A	sl	L	C			6 up
71	Surprising Facts	Chrystie							
127	Swimming	Schiffer	A	sl	L				2-5
120	Tales of Ancient Araby	Mozley			L				k-3
121	Tales of Ancient Egypt	Mozley	A		L		CS		k-3
144	Teaching Machines	Epstein	A	sl	L				7 up
59	Television	Stoddard	A	sl	L	C			4-8
126	Tools	Liberty	A		L				3-5
3	Trains	R Hamilton	A		L	C	CS		3-6
17	Trees	Cormack	A	sl	L	C	CS	H	3 up
78	Tropical Mammals	H Hoke	A		L				4-7
106	The United Nations	E Epstein	A		L	C	CS		4 up
147	Vikings	Rich	A	sl	L				4 up
145	War of 1812	Morris	A						5 up
138	Washington, D. C.	Epstein			L				5 up
117	Water	F C Smith	A		L	C			3-5
32	The Weather	Wyler	A		L	C	CS		4-7
93	West Germany	Lobsenz	A	sl	L	C			5-8
70	The West Indies	Hughes	A		L	C	CS	H	4 up
132	Wild Flowers	Cavanna	A	sl	L				4-6
52	Words	S & B Epstein	A	sl	L	C	CS		5-8
82	World War I	Snyder	A	sl	L	C	CS		6 up
80	World War II	Snyder	A	sl	L	C	CS		6 up

The FIRST BOOK Editions

E1	The Declaration of Independence		A		L		CS		All
E2	The Man Without a Country	Hale	A	sl			CS		All
E3	The Star Spangled Banner						CS		All
E4	A Message to Garcia	Hubbard	New Publication						

ALL are supplied in the Watts Guaranteed Library Binding

ALL are in large, clear type

ALL are fully illustrated—many with over 100 pictures, and in color

ALL checked and double-checked for accuracy, authority, and clarity of text

ALL 7¼ x 8¾ size

KEY TO LISTINGS:

A American Library Association, Booklist

sl Booklist, Small Library Listing

L Library Journal

C H. W. Wilson Company, Children's Catalog

CS Child Study Association of America, Books of the Year for Children

H H. W. Wilson Company, High School Catalog

What they say about
FIRST BOOKS

"Their wide appeal, their broad coverage of varied subject areas, their wide range of significant and timely topics, and their attractive format and illustrations have made them valuable library materials."

MIRIAM PETERSON
Chicago Board of Education

"The format of each book has been superior and the books show that careful attention has been given to design, type, illustration, paper, and binding."

CAROLYN W. FIELD
Philadelphia Public Library

"I have long felt that the FIRST BOOKS developed (by Franklin Watts) were among the important creative contributions made by a publisher in recent decades."

PROF. HAROLD G. SHANE
Indiana University

"I really don't know how we ever ran our school libraries without the FIRST BOOKS!"

ELIZABETH HODGES
Baltimore Board of Education

"In covering a topic thoroughly, these books are like a junior encyclopedia, with an illustrated volume for each subject."

Christian Science Monitor

"Indeed an achievement! The high quality which has been maintained throughout the series is even more remarkable."

RUTH HILL VIGUERS
The Horn Book

"The FIRST BOOKS have made a real contribution in extending the horizons of their readers beyond the interests they knew they had."

JOSETTE FRANK
Child Study Association of America

Write for catalog. Address Dept. Sc

FRANKLIN WATTS, INC. A Division
575 Lexington Avenue   New York 22, N. Y.   of Grolier Incorporated

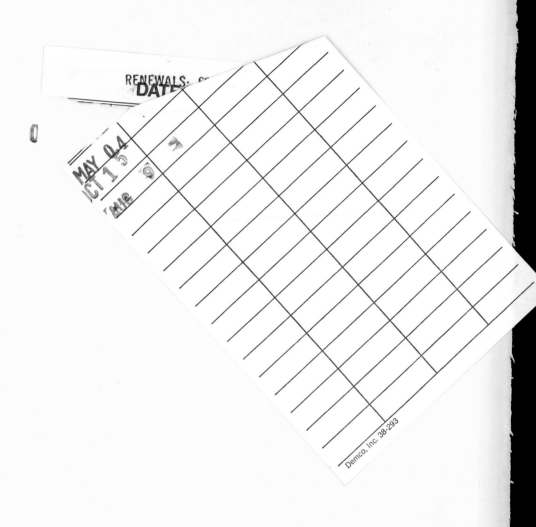